CW00552952

THE LITTLE BOOK
OF THE
SAS

Peter Ratcliffe, DCM

MICHAEL O'MARA BOOKS LIMITED

First published in Great Britain in 2001 by
Michael O'Mara Books Limited
9 Lion Yard, Tremadoc Road
London SW4 7NQ

A CIP catalogue record for this book is available
from the British Library

ISBN 1-85479-887-1

1 3 5 7 9 10 8 6 4 2

Designed and typeset by Martin Bristow

Printed in Australia by McPherson's Printing Group

110 *see* **Land Rover Defender 110**

14 Int 14 Intelligence and Security Company, an undercover detachment deployed by the army in Northern Ireland, 1974–94. Seconded from army units, the men and women of 14 Int, operating in plain clothes, gathered intelligence about suspected **PIRA** (q.v.) members. Hard intelligence was passed for further action to the SAS squadron in Northern Ireland at the time. Also known as 'Det', short for 'the Detachment'; many of its members were either SAS, or SAS-trained

2IC second-in-command

4-tonner Bedford 4-wheel-drive canvas-backed medium truck, used throughout the British Army to transport troops, supplies and equipment. There are specialist versions of the vehicle, and most are equipped with a machine-gun mounting on the cab roof, in which there is a hatch allowing the gunner to fire the weapon

AAM *see* **AIM**

adoo Arabic for enemy: Marxist-backed rebels of the People's Front for the Liberation of the Occupied Arabian Gulf (PFLOAG), operating in Oman, principally **Dhofar** (q.v), to overthrow the Sultan and his government. The adoo were mainly based in, and were supplied and supported by, Oman's southern neighbour, the People's Democratic Republic of Yemen

AF252 official Army Form (hence 'AF'), otherwise known as a charge sheet, on which are recorded the charges a soldier faces and the disciplinary process he will face. *See also* **DCM**; **GCM**; **SUS**

AF 1771 the official Army Form on which a soldier makes claims for expenses; hence a much sought after piece of bumf (and the SAS soldier's favourite form . . .)

Agusta A-109 Italian-designed and built single-rotor, twin-turboshaft light helicopter used by the SAS; several are kept at the Regiment's base in Hereford

AIM air-intercept missile (or air-to-air missile – AAM)

Airborne mug plastic container fitting to the base of the water bottle (also plastic), so as to avoid damage in parachute landings

Airborne stew a mixed-up slop of boiled potatoes, carrots, onions, meat and dry bread, all slung in a stewpot. Served in great dollops, it looks awful and tastes worse, but it's hot, filling and keeps you going

air-marker panel lightweight fabric or plastic-cloth rectangle, usually orange, carried in a soldier's **belt kit** (q.v.) and deployed to indicate to an overflying aircraft where to land or drop its load

Air Troop one of the four troops that make up an SAS **Sabre Squadron** (q.v.). All **badged** (q.v.) members of the SAS are trained parachutists, but members of the Air Troops are specialists, particularly in freefall techniques (*see* **HAHO;**

HALO). Among other skills, they are trained in clandestine entry into enemy territory from the air, and to act as pathfinders for parachute troops jumping after them

AK-47 Soviet-designed, magazine-fed 7.62mm automatic assault rifle, produced in many variants. Built under licence in other communist states, notably China, the former East Germany, Hungary, Poland, and the former Yugoslavia, it is one of the most numerous shoulder weapons in the world. Also known as the Kalashnikov Model 1947, the 'AK' stands for *Avtomat Kalashnikov* (Russian: Kalashnikov automatic) after its designer, Mikhail Timofeyevich Kalashnikov (1919–). The AK-47 was replaced by the 7.62mm AKM, and then by the 5.45mm AK-74, but countless examples are still in service around the world.

AP armour-piercing

ASM air-to-surface missile

A Team the basic 12-man section or patrol of **US Special Forces** (q.v.)

Australian SAS formed in 1964, the Australian Special Air Service Regiment (SASR) was attached to 22 SAS for operations against Indonesian insurgents in Borneo from 1965–6. From 1966 one squadron in rotation served for twelve months with other Australian forces in Vietnam, until all these were withdrawn in 1971. Organized along similar lines to 22 SAS, present SASR establishment includes three **Sabre Squadrons** (q.v.), which rotate in turn in the counter-terrorist role; the troops within the combat squadrons also follow the 22 SAS pattern, and the two units maintain close contacts. *See also* **New Zealand SAS**

badge designed by David **Stirling** (q.v.) in 1941, the famous 'winged dagger' badge of the SAS in fact represents King Arthur's sword Excalibur, the sword of freedom. Cap badges have been of cloth since their inception. *See also* **motto**

badged to be accepted into the SAS, the point at which newly joined members, having passed **Selection**, receive their sand-coloured **berets** with the famous 'winged dagger' **badge** (qq.v.)

bait Dhofari (*see* **Dhofar**) house or native hut (Arabic)

banjo sandwich; *see also* **egg banjo**

banjo, to to beat up or kill; to attack. Probably from slang 'banjo' for frying pan or, in Australian slang, a long-handled shovel, because of the resemblance of these to the musical instrument; frying pans are traditionally represented as being used to belabour someone with

basha shelter for sleeping; hence 'to basha' meaning to get some sleep

basha up, to to prepare for night stop

BATT British Army training team, a euphemism originally used in Oman for the SAS squadron sent to assist in the war against the *adoo* (q.v.);

also used of any SAS team attached to a *firqat* (q.v.) or other pro-government force

battle honours the battle honours of the Special Air Service Regiment, awarded since the Regiment's founding in 1941, are: North-West Europe 1944–45; Benghazi Raid; Tobruk 1941; North Africa 1940–43; Landing in Italy; Sicily 1943; Termoli; Valli di Comacci; Italy 1943–45; Greece 1944–45; Adriatic; Middle East 1943–44; Falkland Islands 1982; Iraq 1991. As the SAS does not have a regimental colour, the battle honours are rarely seen

beat the clock, to to avoid having your name added to those on the **Clock Tower** (q.v.)

belt kit soldier's webbing and attachments, holding much of his personal equipment, ammunition, water bottle etc.

beret the famous sand-coloured (sometimes referred to as 'beige') headgear of the SAS, with its cloth winged-dagger **badge** (q.v.), is issued to

11

each trooper once he has passed **Selection** (q.v.).
Berets are guarded and cared for lovingly; the
author's own served him throughout his twenty-
five years with the Regiment

bergen soldier's rucksack

berm man-made sandbank or dune, usually from
6 to 16 feet high, often with a ditch on the side
facing enemy or unfriendly territory. They
became familiar to the Regiment's patrols during
the Gulf War; the berm along the Iraqi/Saudi-
Arabian border extended in places for many
miles

'Big Four', the number, rank, name and date of
birth – the only information a soldier, and
particularly an SAS soldier, is permitted to give
to his captors when being interrogated

bivvybag waterproof cover, made from Gore-Tex,
for a soldier's sleeping bag or **green maggot**
(q.v.)

black ops operations, generally those carried out

by the **SP team** (q.v.), for which the SAS wear black flame-proof coveralls. *See also* **green ops**

blue-on-blue an incident in which friendly forces mistakenly fire upon each other; a casualty resulting from such an incident. Also known by the euphemism 'friendly fire'

Blue Room building at **Stirling Lines** (q.v.) that was used for briefings of larger numbers of soldiers. It was in fact a substantial hut or shack faced and roofed with corrugated iron ('wriggly tin') and painted blue overall

bluey airmail letter form issued to troops serving in a theatre of operations outside Europe, and used to write home; they pay their own postage, however

Boat Troop one of the four troops that make up an SAS **Sabre Squadron** (q.v.), its principal role is using water as a means of getting ashore from vessels at sea or of infiltrating enemy positions. Members are trained in the use of outboard-powered **Gemini** inflatables or **Rigid Raiders**, **Klepper** (q.v.) canoes and other craft. Training also includes boat-handling, scuba diving, underwater demolitions and water-borne infiltration techniques. Close links are maintained with the **SBS** (q.v.) through training and exercises

Boss slang for anyone in command, whether of a patrol, a troop, or a squadron or larger unit

Bradbury Lines *see* **Stirling Lines**

brat anyone who has been a boy soldier

Bravo Two Zero callsign of an 8-man SAS foot patrol from B Squadron, led by Sergeant 'Andy **McNab**' (q.v.), sent into Iraq during the Gulf War. Discarding advice to take a vehicle and to reduce each man's vast load of equipment and supplies, the patrol was inserted into Iraq by helicopter on the evening of 21 January 1991. On the following day they were **compromised** (q.v.) and forced to fight a running battle with

Iraqi troops to escape, during which they abandoned their **bergens** (q.v.) and wireless set. Despite the **E&E** (q.v.) plan he had filed before leaving, 'McNab' opted to strike north-westwards for the Syrian border, rather than southwards for Saudi Arabia, a safer route, as well as shorter. As a result, rescue helicopters sent out to search their proposed E&E route missed them. During an arduous march the patrol became separated into two groups, 'McNab' with five men, and another group of three, including 'Chris **Ryan**' (q.v.). In the bitterly cold weather one man from each group died of exposure; another from 'McNab's' group was killed in a firefight with Iraqi troops, and all the rest were captured except 'Ryan', who alone made it to Syria and safety. Imprisoned and mistreated by their captors, the four other survivors were eventually repatriated to Britain after the war's end. The bodies of the three dead men – Sergeant Vince Philips, Corporal Steve 'Legs' Lane and Trooper Bob Consiglio – were returned to Britain after the end of the war, and given a full military funeral at **St Martin's Church** (q.v.), Hereford

brew soldiers' slang for any hot drink, but especially a cup of tea

brick basic four-man section or patrol of the SAS, or four-man infantry patrol

Browning High Power 9mm semi-automatic pistol built by the Belgian arms company FN. With a 13-round magazine and considerable stopping power, it has long been the SAS's handgun of choice

Browning M2 US-designed, Second World War-vintage 0.5-inch heavy machine-gun, mounted on some SAS **Land Rover Defender 110s** (q.v.) in the Gulf campaign. An air-cooled, belt-fed weapon with a rate of fire of 450–575 rounds per minute, it is capable of penetrating over 40mm of armour at ranges of more than 800 metres. Also known as the '50-cal', the weapon first saw service with the Regiment in the Western Desert in 1942

buckit mountain or hill (from Malay *bukit*, mountain)

buckshee free; without charge (from Arabic *baksheesh*, ultimately from a Persian word meaning to give)

buddy-buddy system system in use in the SAS, whereby two soldiers act in concert, e.g. in cooking rations, when one will prepare one part of the meal, and the other the rest, or in the jungle, when one will stand guard while the other defecates

bug out, to to leave (a position, firefight etc.) with all speed (originally US slang, often meaning to retreat or even to run away)

Bun Fight, the the Regiment's annual all-ranks Christmas get-together, a buffet meal, lubricated with plenty of beer, held in the cookhouse at Hereford

burmoil 45-gallon steel drum used to transport fuel; often reused for water, which as a result is tainted with the smell and taste of fuel

burnous native goatskin coat; also known to the SAS in the Gulf War as a 'bedou' or 'Al Jouf coat' (*see* **FOB**)

C-130 Hercules long-serving 4-turboprop transport aircraft of great ruggedness, reliability and adaptability, and capable of short takeoffs and landings from grass, scrub, desert and other surfaces besides tarmac. Designed and built by Lockheed in the USA, and in service with, among many others, one of the RAF's Special Forces flights (47 Squadron). *See also* **TLS**

cabal meeting of a small number of people usually chaired by the CO of 22 SAS

cabbage head Royal Marine; so called from the marines' green berets

Calvert, Brigadier Michael, DSO* commissioned into the Royal Engineers in 1933, by the outbreak of war in 1939 Calvert was involved in preparing troops for guerrilla warfare and in training commandos. Posted to Burma in 1942, he worked with Major-General Orde Wingate in establishing the Chindits, units trained to operate behind Japanese lines for extended periods, and went with them on operations, earning the nickname 'Mad Mike'. In March 1945, Calvert, by then commanding a Chindit brigade, left Burma to command the SAS Brigade in Europe, and held the post until the entire unit was disbanded later that year. In 1950 he was asked by the C-in-C, Far East Land Forces, to report on the threat from communist terrorists in Malaya, and as a result was ordered to raise a counter-insurgency unit. The **Malayan Scouts** (q.v.) proved so successful that in 1952 it was re-formed as 22 SAS. Calvert left the army under unhappy circumstances in the 1950s, and thereafter established a reputation as an expert in guerrilla warfare and counter-insurgency, and as a military historian; his account of the Chindit campaign, *Prisoners of Hope* (1952), has become a classic. He was appointed **DSO** (q.v.), and in 1992 visited the Regiment at **Stirling Lines** (q.v.) as its guest of honour. He died in 1999

casevac military abbreviation for casualty evacuation. *See also* **CSAR**

CH-47 Chinook giant twin-turboshaft, twin-rotor transport helicopter, widely in service with the USAF and RAF, and used by RAF Special Forces flights (7 and 18 Squadrons); designed and built by Boeing in the USA, it is generally known by its manufacturer's name of Chinook; its RAF designation was originally HC1, with the uprated aircraft designated HC2 and dedicated Special Forces aircraft HC3

chaff clouds of metal-foil fragments fired from a discharger by a ship, aircraft or other potential target, to confuse the radar of an enemy aircraft, ground station, missile etc.

chalk military term for an aircraft load, varying in size according to the type of aircraft. So called from the **load master's** (q.v.) chalk outline drawn on the hangar floor to show the size of the load

charge sheet *see* **AF252**

Chinese parliament discussion among a group of soldiers, regardless of rank, to agree a plan or course of action. The system is much used in the SAS

Chinook *see* **CH-47**

CILOR cash in lieu of rations: money issued to SAS squadrons, for instance when operating abroad

Claymore mine remotely detonated anti-personnel mine, consisting of an explosive charge in which are embedded hundreds of steel ball bearings. Used for ambushes or to protect a defensive position, Claymores are fired by a sentry from a concealed position when an enemy comes within range. The mines were a favourite of US troops during the Vietnam War, but contrary to what other accounts have said, *no* Claymores were issued to the SAS during the Gulf campaign

click slang for kilometre

Clock Tower the memorial clock at SAS **RHQ** (q.v.) in Hereford, on which are recorded the names of SAS soldiers killed while serving in the Regiment. *See also* **beat the clock**

COBRA Cabinet Office Briefing Room: office used for meetings of senior people from government, the police and the military during major terrorist actions within the UK, or affecting UK nationals

cock, hook and look, to said of an automatic

weapon, e.g. an **M16** (q.v.): to cock the weapon, hook the lever back and examine the chamber to make sure that there is no round in the breech and that the weapon is safe

compo composite: military term for anything intended to last for several days, as 'compo **rations**' (q.v.), a 'compo pack'. The word is generally employed to mean composite rations for use in the field or on exercise

compromised, to be of an individual, unit, covert plan or operation: to be exposed to or discovered by the enemy or other potentially hostile agency, or otherwise to be endangered beyond the point of acceptable risk

confidential report document, also known as the 'pen picture', recording the opinions of the CO and others about a soldier, kept up to date yearly throughout his service career. Each annual report must be shown to its subject, who has to initial it to indicate that he has seen it; he can,

however, appeal to a higher authority if he
disagrees with a particular assessment

contact encounter and firefight with an enemy

CQB close-quarter battle. *See also* **Killing House**

crab member of the Royal Air Force

cross-deck to move personnel and/or stores from
one ship to another by helicopter. During the
Falklands campaign, a Sea King helicopter
cross-decking men of the Regiment's D and G
Squadrons from the carrier HMS *Hermes* (the
flagship of Admiral John 'Sandy' Woodward,
commanding the Task Force) to the assault ship
HMS *Intrepid* crashed into the sea; of the 3 crew
and 27 men aboard 22 lost their lives, the
majority of them SAS

CSAR casevac (q.v.) search and rescue (**SAR**, q.v.)

CSM company sergeant-major, a **WO2** (q.v.)

CSPEP container, straps, personal equipment,
parachutist: a bag, secured with buckles, into
which a soldier's kit is strapped, with his weapon

lashed on top. During the jump the CSPEP is lowered to the end of a line about 15 feet beneath the parachutist, so that it hits the ground before he does

C Squadron, SAS raised in Rhodesia in 1950 to fight in Malaya during the Emergency, this volunteer unit was absorbed into the **Malayan Scouts** (q.v.) and renamed C (Rhodesia) Squadron, retaining that title after the Scouts became 22 SAS in 1952. However, it was disbanded on returning from Malaya later that year, only to be re-formed in 1961 as C Squadron, Rhodesian SAS. It played a major part in combating insurgents during the war in Rhodesia that resulted from the struggle for independence, 1966–80, and in 1978 was redesignated 1 SAS Regiment. When Robert Mugabe's ZANU party won power in 1980 and Rhodesia became Zimbabwe, 1 SAS Regiment was disbanded. *See also* **Sabre Squadrons**

CTR close-target reconnaissance; the final recce carried out just before an operation or assault is launched

DCM (1) Distinguished Conduct Medal: once the highest-ranking gallantry award for **ORs** (q.v.) after the **VC** ([1] q.v.), it is no longer awarded. *See also* **DSO**

DCM (2) district court martial, as distinct from a **GCM** (q.v.)

de la Billière, General Sir Peter, KCB, KBE, DSO, MC* born in 1934, 'DLB' joined the King's Shropshire Light Infantry in 1952, and was then commissioned into the Durham Light Infantry. He joined the SAS as a captain in 1955, and saw active service in Malaya, Oman – where he won the **MC** (q.v.) – Aden and the Radfan, and Borneo (1965; Bar to MC). He commanded A Squadron from 1964–72, and 22 SAS from 1972–4, after which he attended Staff College; he was appointed to the **DSO** (q.v.) in 1976.

After commanding the **BATT** (q.v.) in the Sudan in 1977, he was Director, SAS and Commander, SAS Group from 1979–83, overseeing B Squadron's successful assault on the Iranian Embassy in London (*see* **Princes Gate hostage rescue**) and the Regiment's deployment in the Falklands campaign. From 1984 he held a series of senior posts, being promoted lieutenant-general and appointed KCB. In 1990, on the eve of the Gulf War, he took command of British Forces, Middle East, and was one of the architects of the Coalition victory over Iraq, as well as a crucial ally to the SAS in its struggle for a role in the conflict. He was promoted general and appointed KBE after the Gulf campaign, and retired from active service in 1992. His Gulf War book, *Storm Command* (1992), was the first to break the story of **Bravo Two Zero** and 'Chris **Ryan's**' (qq.v.) escape from Iraq; a second volume of memoirs,

Looking for Trouble (1994), gives an account of DLB's SAS career

Delta Force US First Special Forces Operations Detachment Delta. A counter-terrorist unit formed in the 1970s, Delta Force is the US armed services' equivalent of the SAS, and the two units maintain close contacts

desert boots lightweight leather boot issued to members of the Regiment prior to deployment to desert areas. In fact, during **Operation Storm** (q.v.) members of the Regiment preferred to leave their boots behind and wear them on their return – which meant that girls in Hereford were always able to identify SAS men

'Det' – *see* **14 Int**

dhobi, to to wash clothes; hence 'I've got some dhobi to do'. The word, from Hindi *dhob*, washing, has been in military use since the days of British India

Dhofar southernmost province of the Sultanate of

Oman, to which the SAS were mainly posted during **Operation Storm** (q.v.), 1970–6. The western boundary of Dhofar forms Oman's border with the PDR of Yemen

diggers soldiers' term for knife, fork, spoon. Also known as 'KFS'

DLB SAS nickname for General Sir Peter **de la Billière** (q.v.)

dog tags three metal personal-identification discs worn around the neck by every soldier in the British Army; each is engraved with the soldier's name, army number and blood group. When a soldier is killed or dies from wounds, one tag is left with the body, and the other two are taken by a medical orderly, member of a burial detail etc. and handed in for record-keeping purposes

donkey walloper cavalryman – a member of any of the cavalry regiments or those making up the Royal Armoured Corps, or of the Royal Horse Artillery

double tap two aimed shots fired from a pistol in rapid succession

DPM disruptive-pattern material: fabric printed with camouflage shades and patterns and made up into uniforms etc.

draw and fit SAS/**Para** (q.v.) slang meaning to prepare for a parachute jump; i.e. to draw a parachute and fit the harness

drop short nickname for a Gunner (that is, a member of the Royal Regiment of Artillery). It is in fact the term for an artillery or mortar round that falls short of its target, and which can therefore endanger troops advancing under the cover of the artillery barrage

DS directing staff: those permanent members of a training establishment or course responsible for the programme and for those attending it

D.Sh.K M1938/46 *see* 'Spargan'

DSO Distinguished Service Order: formerly the highest-ranking gallantry award for officers after the **VC** ([1] q.v.), now open to all ranks. The equivalent award for **ORs** (q.v.) was the **DCM** ([1] q.v.); the naval equivalent is the Distinguished Service Cross (DSC)

DZ drop zone: the designated area for a parachute landing. *See also* **DZSO**; **LZ**

DZSO drop-zone safety officer: RAF officer who must be present on the **DZ** (q.v.) on exercise in the UK or abroad

E & E escape and evasion

egg banjo fried-egg sandwich. *See* **banjo**

Egyptian PT in SAS parlance, a soldier's siesta. The term dates from Britain's military involvement in Egypt from the nineteenth century until after the Second World War

elint electronic intelligence: information about an enemy, target etc. gained from electronic surveillance, including information received from satellites. *See also* **humint**; **sigint**

ENDEX end exercise: signal sent to units or

individuals confirming that an exercise or
operation has ended, with immediate effect

EPC Education Promotion Certificate, a qualification which every soldier has to acquire before he
can be promoted sergeant. *See also* **EPCA**

EPCA Education Promotion Certificate,
Advanced: qualification needed by every **NCO**
(q.v.) for higher promotion, including
promotion to commissioned rank. *See also* **EPC**

EW (1) early warning

EW (2) electronic warfare

FAC forward air control or controller: soldier or
soldiers equipped with radio, and often posi-
tioned well forward of a main body of troops, to
guide supporting aircraft on to their targets

fastball something that has to be acted upon
immediately, whether by an individual, a small
group, or an entire SAS squadron, as in 'I'm
handing this over to you – it's a fastball and
you're going to have to get going now'

fast-roping technique for making a rapid descent on to or into a target. It involves sliding fast down a thick rope – the upper end of which is anchored either to a fixed point or to a helicopter – using gloves to protect the hands from rope burn

fat wallet member of the Royal Army Pay Corps unit attached to 22 SAS at Hereford

FAV fast attack vehicle, also known as an LSV (light strike vehicle): small, usually 2-man, 4x4 vehicle consisting of a tubular metal framework and chassis with only minimal bodywork, but designed to mount a considerable weight of weaponry. Faster than the **Land Rover Defender 110s** (q.v.), the SAS tested FAVs in the desert prior to the Gulf War. In the event, problems, subsequently resolved, with reliability and robustness led to their not being used in Iraq

FEBA forward edge of battle area

FIBUA fighting in built-up areas: self-explanatory term used mainly of training for operations in Northern Ireland

'fighting knife' one of the enduring myths about the Regiment, bolstered by references to knives in several books by former SAS members. There is, in fact, no such thing in the British Army as a 'fighting knife', and no unit uses such knives (other than bayonets) in combat or on active service. The only knives issued are small clasp knives. Some SAS soldiers carry slightly larger knives (*see* **Leatherman; Swiss Army knife**), but only for ordinary purposes. There are no instruction courses in the SAS involving the use of knives – the only time knives are involved is during unarmed-combat instruction on defence against an antagonist armed with a blade. The myth persists, however

firqat Arabic name (literally, 'company') for an irregular unit formed, mainly from **SEPs**, to

combat the ***adoo*** operating in Oman, especially
Dhofar (qq.v.)

flash bang also known as a stun grenade: an SAS
invention, on detonation these devices emit a
blinding flash of magnesium coupled with a loud
report, temporarily stunning and disorienting
opponents, but without causing shrapnel or blast
damage. *See also* **Mogadishu**

FMB forward mounting base: a unit's initial base
during an operation, from which it will move
forward to the **FOB** (q.v.); for the SAS in the
Gulf War the forward mounting base was at
Victor in the **UAE** (q.v.)

FOB forward operating base: for the SAS in the
Gulf War, this was at Al Jouf in north-western
Saudi Arabia, some 150 kilometres south of the
Iraqi border

FOO forward observation officer: officer or NCO
trained in spotting the fall of shot from mortars
or artillery; he will often man an **FOP** (q.v.)

ahead of the main body of assault troops, from which he will call back corrections to guns' or mortars' aim by radio

FOP forward observation post, manned by an **FOO** (q.v.)

Free Beer codeword formerly used to order SAS soldiers to return to **RHQ** (q.v.) at once. It was changed after an incident in which the mother of a trooper on leave failed to pass on the message, on the grounds that her son had had 'far too much beer over Christmas'

friendly fire *see* **blue-on-blue**

galley cookhouse (naval; from the Falklands campaign)

GCM general court martial. *See also* **DCM** (2)

Gemini rubber inflatable boat, powered by an outboard motor, and used by SAS **Boat Troops**, as well as by the **SBS** (qq.v.)

geysh Arabic word meaning 'army', used in Oman of the regular troops of the Sultan of Oman's

Armed Forces. A high proportion of the geysh were Baluchis, and effectively mercenaries in the Sultan's employ

gimpy *see* **GPMG**

ginger beer member of the Corps of Royal Engineers

glasshouse British Army gaol; the main prison, known simply as 'the Glasshouse', is at Colchester

gobbin Guardsman; anyone from the Brigade of Guards

GPMG general-purpose machine-gun: the British version of the Belgian-designed and built FN MAG, the 'gimpy' (as it is affectionately nicknamed) is a 7.62mm belt-fed, air-cooled machine-gun designated L7 in the British Army, and with a cyclic rate of fire of 750–1,000 rounds per minute; rugged and reliable, and capable of being used in the sustained-fire role, it has been in service for many years

GPS global positioning system: hand-held electronic device that receives information from a number of orbiting satellites, so allowing its operator to pinpoint his position to within a few yards at any time of day and in any conditions. An invaluable navigational aid, the SAS used the Magellan GPS during the Gulf campaign. *See also* **Trimpack**

Green Army SAS term for the rest of the British Army; that is, every non-Special Forces unit

Green Berets *see* **US Special Forces**

Green Death the **SBS** (q.v.), from the marines' green berets

Green Machine the Royal Marines, from their green berets; *see also* **Maroon Machine**

green maggot sleeping bag

green ops operations for which the SAS wear normal **DPM** (q.v.) combat fatigues. *See also* **black ops**

Green Slime *see* **I Corps**

GSG9 *Grenzschutzgruppe* (Border Protection Group) 9: German police anti-terrorist unit set up in the wake of the **Munich Olympics massacre** (q.v.) of September 1972. GSG 9 maintains close operational and training links with the SAS. When the German unit successfully stormed the hijacked aircraft at **Mogadishu** (q.v.) in 1977, two SAS men were present as advisers; similarly, during the **Princes Gate hostage rescue** (q.v.) in 1980, the head of GSG9 acted as an adviser to the SAS

GSM General Service Medal: awarded to soldiers for taking part in a campaign for which a clasp has been issued. *See also* **LSGCM**

HAHO high altitude, high opening: SAS-developed parachuting technique, involving jumping from above 25,000 feet and immediate opening of the chute. The parachutist can then glide for a considerable distance using a special controllable chute. *See also* **HALO**

HALO high altitude, low opening: SAS-developed technique for inserting patrols by parachute, involving freefall from above 25,000 feet to about 3,500 feet at night and 2,500 in daylight.

hard arrest method used by soldiers when operating in aid to the civil power in apprehending, without shooting, suspects known to be unarmed. The SAS make the arrests armed with batons, though carrying firearms in case a suspect takes up a weapon, as was the case with the Peterhead Gaol siege in October 1987

hard routine routine employed on clandestine operations and when close to the enemy, as well as during training exercises, involving no noise, no smoking, and no cooking. SAS troops in covert **OPs** (q.v.) have been known to follow a hard routine for a week or more

heads lavatory (naval; from the Falklands campaign)

headshed SAS colloquialism for any person or body in authority; thus a 'headsheds' meeting' for a large mobile patrol might be a meeting of all officers and **SNCOs**, while the 'headshed' at **Stirling Lines** would be the CO and senior **RHQ** (qq.v.) officers and NCOs. The word derives from the Malayan campaign of the 1950s, and has its origins in the watersheds so frequently encountered in the Regiment's operations against the communist insurgents there

Hercules *see* **C-130**

Hereford Gun Club, Hereford Hooligans the SAS. *See also* **nicknames**

hexamine solid fuel in the form of small, white rectangular blocks or tablets, used in soldiers' portable stoves, and more generally in miniature camping stoves

HLS helicopter landing strip. *See also* **TLS**

holsters the SAS use two types, shoulder and hip

holsters. Each is designed to hold a concealed 9mm semi-automatic pistol, and they are used when members are performing VIP-protection or bodyguarding duties, or are on clandestine operations

housewife (usu. pron. 'huzziff') sewing and mending kit issued to every soldier, containing needles, thread, thimble, buttons, pins, scissors etc.

humint human intelligence: information about an enemy, target etc. gained as a result of observation by operatives. *See also* **elint; sigint**

I Corps Intelligence Corps: there is an I Corps unit permanently attached to 22 SAS. Known derisively in the rest of the army as 'Green Slime', from the colour of their berets

IMS instinctive method of shooting, designed to teach soldiers to shoot rapidly and accurately with a pistol without taking aim

Ingram 9mm magazine-fed, fixed-firing-pin

submachine-gun with an exceptionally high rate of fire. Also known as the MAC10

Intel, intel an Intelligence unit or members of that unit; intelligence in general as transmitted to troops in the field

Intelligence Corps *see* **I Corps**

IO Intelligence Officer

IVCP illegal **VCP** (q.v.): often set up in Northern Ireland by members of **PIRA** (q.v.) as a means of controlling or intimidating local populations

jebali inhabitant of the *jebel* area of **Dhofar** (qq.v.)

jebel also *djebel*: Arabic for hill or mountain; specifically, the mountain area of **Dhofar** in which the *adoo* (qq.v.) mainly operated

jet jockey RAF fighter pilot

JNCO *See* **SNCO/JNCO**

JSIU Joint Services Interrogation Unit: a branch of **I Corps** (q.v.), the JSIU assists the SAS in **RTI** (q.v.) training, in certain types of exercise, and during the **E&E** phase of **Selection** (qq.v.).

On operations and in wartime, JSIU interrogators are attached to SAS units on active service

jungle boots leather boot equipped with canvas ventilation pieces and eyelets wide enough to let water drain out, but small enough not to let leeches in. Also fitted with a steel plate in the sole, to protect the wearer in the event of his treading on a **punji stick** (q.v.)

Katyusha Soviet-designed and built unguided short-range rocket, often fired from multiple launchers. Deployed by the *adoo* (q.v.) to bombard SAS positions and other targets in Oman

Killing House, the purpose-built indoor firing range at the Regiment's base in Hereford, in which SAS soldiers practise live firing when carrying out simulated hostage-rescue operations; properly, the Close-Quarter Battle House

Kite sight British-designed and built lightweight

weapon-aiming system, capable of being fitted
to most combat rifles and light anti-tank
weapons; permits the firer to aim even in total
darkness.

Klepper collapsible 2-man canoe used by SAS
Boat Troops and the **SBS** (qq.v.)

knives *see* 'fighting knife'; **Leatherman; Swiss
Army knife**

Kremlin, the SAS nickname for Regimental
Headquarters in Hereford. *See* **RHQ**

L16 the standard-issue mortar of the British Army,
the L16A1 is an 81mm weapon capable of
delivering different rounds – high-explosive,
phosphorus, smoke, illumination – accurately at
ranges of more than 5.5 kilometres. Weighing
some 35 kilos all up, it is carried on SAS
vehicles; its HE round weighs in at 4.26 kilos,
making the L16 a formidable support weapon

Land Rover Defender 110 the SAS version of the
110 is a custom-built long-wheelbase (110 inch/

279cm) 4x4 vehicle deployed on active service
by mobile patrols. Sometimes also known as a
'pinky' (q.v.), or more usually as a '110'. The
short-wheelbase version, the Land Rover
Defender 90 (90-inch/229-centimetre
wheelbase; sometimes known as a 'dinky'), is
also used by the Regiment, and both are in
service with many other units of the armed
forces; a stretched version, the 130, with a
squared-off enclosed body, is in service as an
ambulance and as an artillery tractor. The
Regiment's **SP team** (q.v.) deploys Range Rovers
for counter-terrorist operations

LAW light anti-tank weapon

LAW66 shoulder-fired 66mm **LAW** (q.v.),
    deployed by the SAS in the Falklands campaign

LAW80 shoulder-fired 80mm **LAW** (q.v.),
    deployed by the SAS in the Gulf War

lead scout the soldier selected to guide the rest of
    his patrol, choosing the route, navigating,

maintaining pace and direction and keeping a close watch for enemy forces, potential ambushes, natural hazards, obstacles etc. In a four-man patrol or **brick** (q.v.) the order of march would be: lead scout, patrol commander or **PC** (q.v.), no. 3, and **tail-end Charlie** (q.v.)

Leatherman trade name for any of several versions of a compact pocket combination tool including pliers, knife blades, screwdrivers, openers, saw etc., all of which fold up into the handles. The US-made tool comes in a pouch that can be fixed to a belt. Not an issue item, but many SAS soldiers buy their own. *See also* **'fighting knife'; Swiss Army knife**

'Lili Marlene' regimental slow march of the SAS.

LOA local overseas allowance: extra money paid to soldiers when deployed abroad. Also stands for 'leave of absence'

load master on transport aircraft, the RAF NCO who has responsibility for loading and unloading; he has complete control while the aircraft is on the ground, and pilots, however senior, cannot take off without his say so

locstat to record and save the actual coordinates of a fixed feature, position or target

loop line nylon cord, some 30 feet long, with loops at each end, and carried by SAS patrols; immensely strong, they can be quickly joined to make longer lines, and can even be used to tow vehicles

LS landing strip. *See also* **HLS; TLS**

LSGCM Long Service and Good Conduct Medal: awarded to soldiers after fifteen years' service without a blemish (or, as old soldiers say, after fifteen years of undetected crime). *See also* **GSM**

LSV *see* **FAV**

LUP lying-up place

LZ landing zone: the designated area for a landing by helicopter or fixed-wing aircraft. *See also* **DZ**

M16 the American-designed and built Colt M16

(earlier designations were Colt AR-22 or Armalite) entered service with the US armed services in the late 1950s and, like the **AK-47** (q.v.), is now one of the most widely used assault rifles in the world. A fully automatic weapon of 5.56mm calibre and built largely of aluminium and plastic, it is tough, reliable and light. It was first used by the SAS in the Borneo campaign of 1963–6, and increasingly adopted by the Regiment in the ensuing twenty years; it is now the standard-issue rifle of the SAS, which prefers it to the British-designed and built 5.56mm **SA80** (q.v.) assault rifle with which the rest of the British Army is equipped. SAS soldiers often use M16s fitted with the M203 40mm grenade launcher fitted beneath the barrel

M79 single-shot 40mm grenade launcher, used by the SAS on **Operation Storm** (q.v.) in Oman

M203 *see* **M16**

Malayan Scouts former name for what eventually

became 22 SAS, established as a counter-insurgency unit during the Malayan Emergency, 1948–60 (the Regiment had been disbanded in 1945, at the end of the Second World War). Operating from 1951, and despite initial problems, the Scouts proved so successful against communist terrorists in Malaya that its three squadrons, A, B and C, were incorporated into 22 SAS on the latter's formation in 1952. *See also* **C Squadron**; **Calvert**; **nicknames**

'March of the Belgian Paratroopers' regimental quick march of the SAS

Maroon Machine, Maroon Fighting Machine the Parachute Regiment, so called from their famous red berets. *See also* **Green Machine**

matlo member of the Royal Navy (from French *matelot*, sailor)

MC Military Cross: gallantry award formerly open only to officers and senior warrant officers, but now awarded to all ranks

'McNab', Sergeant 'Andy', DCM, MM pseudonym of a former SAS staff sergeant who wrote the bestselling *Bravo Two Zero* (1993), an account of the patrol (*see* **Bravo Two Zero**) that he commanded behind Iraqi lines during the Gulf War. 'McNab' passed **Selection** (q.v.) at the second attempt in 1984, having begun his career in the Royal Green Jackets, with which he won the **MM** in Northern Ireland (q.v.). Awarded the **DCM** ([1] q.v.) for his service in Iraq, he left the Regiment and the army in the year in which his book was published. He is now a bestselling author of action novels based on his SAS experience. *See also* **'Ryan', Corporal 'Chris'**

Mess dress uniform worn by all ranks for formal occasions such as Mess dinners etc. The Mess dress of the SAS is unique in the British Army, consisting as it does of ordinary evening dress of black dinner jacket and dress trousers, worn with bow tie and cummerbund in the regimental colour (light blue), miniature decorations and regimental cufflinks

MID Mention in Despatches

Milan wire-guided anti-tank missile system deployed by some SAS mobile patrols during the Gulf campaign. At 35 kilos in weight the system is too heavy to be carried by foot patrols, but mounted on the rollbar of a **Land Rover Defender 110** (q.v.), proved devastatingly effective against both mobile targets and fixed defences; its sighting aid, **MIRA** (q.v.), also proved invaluable. The 6.65kg missile has a range of 2,000 metres and can penetrate armour up to 106cm in thickness. Milan first demonstrated its worth in action during the Falklands campaign of 1982

Minimi designed and built by the Belgian arms concern FN, this 5.56mm air-cooled light machine-gun was used by some SAS patrols in the Gulf campaign. With a cyclic rate of fire of

750–1,000 rounds per minute and capable of being fed either by belt or a box magazine, the Minimi can also take the standard **M16** (q.v.) magazine; at 6.8kg it is light enough to be carried by foot patrols

MIRA Milan infrared attachment, a sighting device fitted to the **Milan** (q.v.) missile system. Primarily a night sight, MIRA can be detached from the missile housing and used as a hand-held sighting/detection aid, in which role it proved itself with SAS mobile patrols during the Gulf campaign

Mk19 US-designed and built fully automatic 40mm grenade launcher, mounted on some SAS **Land Rover Defender 110s** (q.v.). Belt fed and air cooled, the Mk19 (also called M19) has a rate of fire of up to 375 rounds per minute and an effective range of 1,600 metres; the variety of grenades it can handle includes high-explosive, smoke and armour-piercing

MM Military Medal: a gallantry award for other ranks, it is no longer awarded. Instead, the **MC** (q.v.) is now open to all ranks

Mobility Troop one of the four troops that make up an SAS **Sabre Squadron** (q.v.), its members are trained in using cross-country vehicles – notably the heavily armed **Land Rover Defender 110s** (q.v.) – for deep-penetration patrols behind enemy lines, long-range reconnaissance, hit-and-run raids etc. Training includes driving in all kinds of terrain and conditions, use of a wide range of weapons and vehicles (including motorcycles and **FAVs** [q.v.]), maintenance and repair, night driving using **PNGs** (q.v.), navigation, and many other skills

MoD Ministry of Defence

Modplod derogatory term for Ministry of Defence Police, especially those who guard and carry out camp security at the SAS base in Hereford

Mogadishu name generally given to the successful storming of a hijacked Lufthansa Boeing 737 aircraft at Mogadishu airport in the Sudan, 1977. The assault was carried out by the West German (now German) **GSG9** (q.v.) anti-terrorist unit, but two SAS members were also present as advisers. The operation also marked the first use in action of stun grenades (*see* **flash bang**), an SAS invention

monkey member of the Corps of Royal Military Police. *See also* **redcaps**

motto 'Who Dares Wins', selected by David **Stirling** (q.v.) when he established the Regiment in 1941

Mountain Troop one of the four troops that make up an SAS **Sabre Squadron** (q.v.), these are the mountain and Arctic warfare specialists. All members are expert skiers and climbers, and are trained in survival techniques for conditions of extreme cold and widely differing terrain, as well as in techniques for assisting units from other troops, or even an entire squadron, up a cliff or other obstacle by means of a fixed climb. The Mountain Troops are also responsible for ski training within the Regiment

MP5 9mm, magazine-fed submachine-gun designed and built by the German concern Heckler & Koch, and available in several variants. The various weapons in the MP5 series have been the SAS's preferred submachine-guns for many years

MSR main supply route: major roads traversing Iraq, principally those from Jordan to Baghdad; some are metalled. One of the prime tasks of the SAS patrols operating in Iraq during the Gulf War was to watch the MSRs and report movements of troops, transport and, especially, mobile **Scud** (q.v.) launchers

MTO motor transport officer

Munich Olympics massacre in September 1972,

Palestinian terrorists of the Black September group stormed the Olympic Village on the outskirts of Munich, killed or wounded several members of the Israeli team, and seized 9 others as hostages. With Israel's categorical refusal to consider terrorist demands, the West German government ordered a rescue attempt. Poorly equipped and trained for operations against hardened terrorists, the German police badly bungled the attempt, and all 9 hostages were killed; 3 terrorists survived and were captured. As a result of the disaster, the West German government ordered the establishment of what is now **GSG9** (q.v.)

NAAFI Navy, Army and Air Force Institutes: the organization which, for decades, has provided the British armed forces with shops, canteens, and other services. An earlier generation of soldiers claimed the acronym stood for 'Never 'Ave Any Fags In'

Naps tablets issued during the Gulf War to Coalition troops, to counteract the effect of possible enemy **NBC** (q.v.) measures

NATO planks wooden cross-country (*langlauf*) skis that used to be issued to all NATO troops, including British forces; heavy and unwieldy, they were not popular with troops, and have now been replaced with Bushwhacker skis

NBC nuclear, biological and chemical, as in 'NBC warfare'; generally used of the protective NBC suits and headgear issued to all servicemen during the Gulf campaign, and of NBC precautionary measures, such as injections and tablets

New Zealand SAS originally formed in 1955 as a single squadron for service in the Malayan Emergency (*see* **Malayan Scouts**), the NZSAS Squadron was disbanded on leaving Malaya in 1957, only to be re-formed in 1959. In 1962, after service in Thailand with **US Special**

Forces (q.v.), the squadron was redesignated 1 Ranger Squadron, NZSAS, and from 1965–6 detachments served on six-month rotation in Borneo under command of 22 SAS. NZSAS soldiers served 6-month tours in Vietnam from 1968 until withdrawal in 1971, rotating through a single troop maintained in-country. The squadron was then redesignated 1 New Zealand SAS Group, and now has an establishment of two **Sabre Squadrons** (q.v.) and ancillary units. Like the **Australian SAS** (q.v.), it maintains close contacts with 22 SAS

nicknames nicknames for the Regiment among the rest of the army/services include: the Artists (from its former incarnation as the Artists' Rifles); the Cloak-and-Dagger Regiment; F Company; the Hereford Gun Club/Hereford Hooligans; the **Malayan Scouts**; the Pilgrims, from the lines of James Elroy Flecker's poem *The Golden Journey to Samarkand*, beginning 'We are the Pilgrims, Master', which are engraved on the memorial **Clock Tower** (q.v.) at the Regiment's HQ in Hereford; **the Regiment** (q.v.); **Sass** (q.v.); Saturday Afternoon Soldiers (used especially of the **TA** [q.v.] units, 21 and 23 SAS); Saturdays and Sundays; the Scandinavian Air Service; Slow and Stupid; Soft and Simple; the Sports and Social; the Stars and Stripes; Sugar and Spice; Sweet and Sour. SAS **Selection** (q.v.) has the nickname Savage and Sadistic. *See also* **SAS**

ninja term used by members of 264 Signal Regiment (*see* **scaly**) to describe an SAS soldier

No. 2 dress uniform worn on parade by all warrant officers, NCOs and **ORs** (q.v.); **WO1s** (q.v.) wear a Sam Browne with it. *See also* **Service dress**

OC officer commanding

O-group orders group: a formal briefing given by a commander before an operation to subordinate commanders, who are tasked with passing the relevant information on to their own subordinates

OP observation post. *See also* **FOP**

Operation Storm codename for SAS involvement in Britain's then secret war against Marxist-backed insurgents (*see* **adoo**) in the Sultanate of Oman, 1970–6. *See also* **BATT**

ops waistcoat waistcoat with front pouches issued to SAS soldiers and used in place of a **bergen** (q.v.) when operating in a light role

OR other rank: every soldier who does not hold commissioned rank

orbat order of battle

Palud-R-Inn Club ironical nickname for the **NAAFI** (q.v.) at the SAS barracks in Hereford (from the anti-malaria drug Paludrine, long familiar to servicemen)

Para, the Paras a member or members of the Parachute Regiment, or that regiment itself

parang the SAS's term for a machete (from Malay *parang*, a heavy broad-bladed knife). Parangs are carried by all members of the Regiment when deployed in jungle

Part 1 orders general orders issued by **RHQ** (q.v.) to squadrons and departments. *See also* **squadron orders**

Patriot MIM-104 Patriot: US-built **SAM** (q.v.) specifically designed to destroy incoming enemy **SSMs** (q.v.). During the Gulf War, Patriot was used against Iraqi **Scud** (q.v.) missiles to considerable effect both in Saudi Arabia and in Israel

PC patrol commander

PE plastic explosive

pen picture *see* **confidential report**

permanent cadre the permanent establishment of 22 SAS at its base in Hereford. When a soldier goes on to the permanent cadre – usually after about four years' service with the Regiment –

he severs all promotion ties with his original unit

PFLOAG Popular Front for the Liberation of the Occupied Arabian Gulf. *See adoo*

Pilgrims, the the SAS's regimental rugby football team, so called from the lines of verse inscribed on the **Clock Tower** (q.v.). *See also* **nicknames**

pinky term used for SAS Land Rovers, short for 'Pink Panther', a name given to the Regiment's patrol vehicles when they were painted in a pink desert camouflage. *See also* **Land Rover Defender 110**

PIRA Provisional IRA: the 'provisional wing' of the Irish Republican Army; also known as 'Provos' or 'stickies'

PJI parachute jump instructor: an RAF NCO who supervises recruits' parachute training

PMC President of the Mess Committee, usually the **RQMS** (q.v.) for the Sergeants' Mess

PNGs passive night-vision goggles

pot soldiers' slang for a helmet

prayers daily/weekly meeting of SAS squadron members or Regimental Headquarters (*see* **RHQ**)

prime time SAS nickname, dating from the 1970s, for free time which, if there were no operations, training or courses, members of the Regiment were permitted to spend as they wished, provided they remained within reach of **RHQ** (q.v.). *See also* **Free Beer**

Princes Gate hostage rescue (also known as the 'Iranian Embassy siege') on the morning of 30 April 1980 six heavily armed Arab terrorists seized the Iranian Embassy in Princes Gate, London, taking 26 hostages, whom they threatened to kill if their demands were not met. The area around the embassy was evacuated and sealed, and the police began hostage negotiations almost at once. Meanwhile, the SAS had been alerted and the advance party of the **SP**

team (q.v.) dispatched, covertly establishing itself in a building next door to the embassy. Despite police negotiators' efforts, by 5 May the situation within the embassy had become dangerously tense. In the early afternoon two shots were heard from inside the building; three more were heard some hours later, after which the body of a hostage was pushed out. As a result, control of the situation was formally passed from the police to the SAS at 1907 hours. At 1923 hours several 4-man units simultaneously breached the embassy with explosive charges from three directions, abseiling from the roof on to the front and rear balconies or down through the skylight. Throwing stun grenades (*see* **flash bang**), they burst in through windows and systematically cleared the rooms, killing four of the terrorists (a fifth was killed by a sniper) and hustling their captives out. One hostage was killed and two wounded by one of the terrorists before the SAS reached the room, and the sixth terrorist was discovered hiding among the evacuated hostages and arrested. The charges had set the building alight and one SAS man was burned when he became tangled in his abseiling equipment – the Regiment's only casualty. The operation, which lasted just seventeen minutes, did more to establish the public perception of the SAS than any other single factor

PTI physical training instructor

Pucara an Argentinian-designed and built twin turboprop close-support/counter-insurgency/reconnaissance aircraft, the FMA IA-58 Pucara was deployed by the Argentinian Air Force during the Falklands campaign; the SAS destroyed six Pucaras on the ground at Pebble Island, and shot down another with a **Stinger** (q.v.) missile

PUFO pack up and fuck off. *See also* **ENDEX**

pulk one-man sledge used by members of the **Mountain Troops** (q.v.); it is drawn by means of a fixed metal harness

punji stick small sharpened bamboo stake with one end set in the ground and the tip, which is usually coated with human excrement or other infective matter, set upwards to puncture the boot and foot of anyone unwary enough to tread on it. Much favoured by the Viet Cong during the Vietnam War, who would often dig concealed 'punji pits' full of such stakes. *See also* **jungle boot**

PX Post Exchange: US armed forces equivalent of the British **NAAFI** (q.v.)

QM Quartermaster: officer of a battalion or regiment responsible for the entire unit's logistics and supply scales

R & R rest and recuperation during operations

rations the SAS is provided with three basic types of field rations: the 24-hour ration pack, the

4-man ration box, and the 10-man ration box.
The 4- and 10-man ration boxes provide those
numbers of men with food for 24 hours, but
obviously a 4-man box could sustain 2 men for
48 hours, or a 10-man box 2 men for 5 days.
The 24-hour packs contain 'boil-in-the-bag'
rations, while the boxes are made up mainly of
tinned food; all will contain lavatory paper,
matches, tea and coffee, and sweets. Typical
menus would include a selection from the
following:

24-hour ration packs –

breakfast: bacon grill, corned-beef hash,
   hamburger and beans

lunch: bacon grill, chocolate bars, hardtack
   biscuits

evening: Lancashire hotpot. The rations are
   dropped into water boiled on a **Peak stove**
   (q.v.), and the water is then used for making
   tea or coffee (*see* **brew**)

4- and 10-man ration boxes –

    breakfast: bacon grill, oatmeal blocks, **compo** (q.v.) sausages, baked beans, jam

    lunch: corned beef, pilchards, salmon, cake, chocolate bars

    evening: rice, mixed vegetables, carrots, peas, stewed steak and onions, chicken supreme, chicken curry, rice pudding, fruit. Almost everything is tinned – even the chocolate bars, jam and cake; the tin containing the chocolate bars also contains boiled sweets and matches.

RCID remote-controlled initiation device: triggering mechanism for an explosive device, allowing the firer to detonate the charge from a distance. A favourite of **PIRA** (q.v.)

RE Corps of Royal Engineers. *See also* **ginger beer**

Red Machine the Parachute Regiment. *See also* **Green Machine**; **Maroon Machine**

'Red on'/'Green on' said in reference to the

lamps inside an aircraft which are illuminated in turn just before a parachute jump. When the **load master** (q.v.) calls 'Red on' it means 'prepare to jump'; 'Green on' means 'Go!' and is a direct order

redcap member of the Corps of Royal Military Police. *See also* **monkey**

Regiment, the the Special Air Service Regiment

REME Corps of Royal Electrical and Mechanical Engineers

REMF rear-echelon motherfucker: US armed-services term for base troops, now in use in the British Army

resup resupply: that is, the delivery of rations, ammunition, water, fuel, replacement equipment etc. – and sometimes fresh food or personnel – to troops operating in the field. Often effected by helicopter, although in one legendary operation during the Gulf War a convoy of SAS trucks and Land Rovers (*see* **Land Rover**

Defender 110) drove more than 100 miles behind enemy lines to resupply the Regiment's mobile patrols operating in Iraq

Rhodesian SAS *see* **C Squadron, SAS**

RHQ Regimental Headquarters: since 1960, 22 SAS RHQ has been in Hereford. *See also* **Stirling Lines**

'Ride of the Valkyrie' regimental quick march of the Parachute Regiment

Rigid Raider shallow-draft, outboard-motor-powered assault boat used by SAS **Boat Troops** and by the **SBS** (qq.v.). Older versions are built from glass-fibre, but the latest types use lighter, if more expensive, materials. The design of the bow and the shallow draft allow the boat to be run up sloping beaches etc. at full power

rock ape member of the RAF Regiment

Rodney mildly pejorative term for an officer, similar to **Rupert** (q.v.)

ROE rules of engagement. *See also* **yellow card**

RQMS regimental quartermaster sergeant, a **WO2** (q.v.)

RSM Regimental Sergeant-Major, a **WO1** (q.v.); sometimes referred to as 'rasm'

RSO regimental signals officer

RTI resistance to interrogation; training course run by the **JSIU** during **Selection** (qq.v.)

RTM ready to move

RTU-ed returned to unit: the fate most dreaded by candidates for or members of the SAS. It usually takes effect immediately, and sees the soldier in question sent back to the regiment or corps from which he has come; however, no official stigma attaches to being RTU-ed

RUC Royal Ulster Constabulary

rum ration although long since discontinued in the Royal Navy, rum is still issued to SAS or other soldiers when engaged in arduous duties

Rupert mildly derogatory soldier's term for an officer. *See also* **Rodney**

RV rendezvous. *See also* **ERV**

'Ryan', Corporal 'Chris', MM pseudonym of a former SAS corporal who wrote the bestselling *The One That Got Away* (1995), the only member of the disastrous **Bravo Two Zero** (q.v.) patrol to avoid death or capture. His epic 7-day, 8-night journey through enemy territory on foot from the point at which the patrol became separated to the Syrian border and safety – 186 miles in all – ranks as one of the greatest escapes of all time; he was awarded the **MM** (q.v.) after the end of the Gulf War. Born in 1961, and a former **TA** (q.v.) soldier with 23 SAS, which he had first unofficially joined as a 16-year-old, Ryan passed Selection for the regular SAS in 1984. He left the Regiment and the army in 1994; like 'Andy **McNab**' (q.v.), he too is now a bestselling author of action novels based on his SAS experience

Sabre Squadrons name given to the four combat squadrons of 22 SAS: A, B, D and G Squadrons. There is no C Squadron, since that designation went to what became 1 Rhodesian SAS (*see* **C Squadron, SAS**), nor an E or F Squadron. G Squadron was established in 1965 around a cadre of former members of Guards Independent Parachute Company who had served with the SAS in Borneo – hence the 'G' designation. The **Australian SAS** and **New Zealand SAS** (qq.v.) also have Sabre Squadrons. *See also* **Air Troop; Boat Troop; Mobility Troop; Mountain Troop**

SA80 British-designed and built 5.56mm magazine-fed fully automatic assault rifle: currently the standard-issue rifle of the British Army (but not the SAS, which favours the lighter and more reliable US-built **M16** [q.v.])

St Martin's the Parish Church of St Martin in Ross Road, Hereford, where many SAS soldiers killed in action or during training are buried in a regimental plot in the churchyard. In the church there is also a stained-glass window presented by and dedicated to the Regiment

SAM surface-to-air missile

SAM7 Soviet-built shoulder-launched **SAM** (q.v.), very widely distributed to satellite nations and Soviet-backed insurgents, and encountered by the SAS during the war in Oman through its use by the *adoo* (q.v.) against aircraft of the RAF and the Sultan of Oman's Air Force. A crude, inaccurate and unreliable weapon, it nevertheless presented a considerable potential threat

sandy bottoms giving your **brew** (q.v.) to someone to finish (naval; from the Falklands campaign)

sangar man-made breastwork or bunker, partially excavated, but with walls built up from the ground using rocks and sandbags (originally a Pashto word adopted by the British Army in the nineteenth century)

SAR search and rescue. *See also* **CSAR**

SARBE *see* **TACBE**

SAS initials of 22 Special Air Service. Within the regiment, also used as an abbreviation for Speed – Aggression – Surprise; Silence and Stealth. *See also* **nicknames**

SAS poncho rectangle of thin, lightweight waterproof fabric, used to make a shelter for a **basha** (q.v.) etc. Unique to the Regiment, the SAS version differs from the British-Army-issue poncho in having no central hole or hood. Small enough to be rolled up and carried in a soldier's **belt kit** (q.v.), it measures some 2x3 metres when unrolled

Sass, the Sass term occasionally used in the **Green Army** (q.v.) for the SAS; it is never used by members of the Regiment. *See also* **nicknames**

satcoms satellite communications; satellite-link telephone. Also called satlink

satlink *see* **satcoms**

SBS Special Boat Service (formerly Squadron), Royal Marines: in some respects the SAS's sister service although, as its name suggests, geared more towards maritime/amphibious operations. It was originally established during the Second World War as a sub-unit of the SAS

Scale A parade mandatory parade for all ranks, without exception

scaly SAS term for a member of 264 Signal Regiment attached to 22 SAS at Hereford. *See also* **ninja**

sched radio schedule (pron. 'sked'): the schedule that provides operators in the field with times and frequencies for radio transmissions

Scud antiquated Soviet-designed and built intermediate-range **SSM** ([2] q.v.), deployed by Iraq during the Gulf War against targets in Israel and Saudi Arabia. Although inaccurate, Scud can carry conventional, biological, chemical or nuclear warheads, and can be fired from mobile, as well as fixed, launch sites, which are difficult to locate by aerial reconnaissance; furthermore, Iraqi engineers had considerably extended its range and marginally improved its crude guidance system, making it still a weapon to be feared. *See also* **MSR; Patriot**

SEALS Special Forces unit of the US Navy, the acronym standing for 'Sea, Air, Land'; roughly equivalent to the **SBS** (q.v.). A SEAL team is attached to **Delta Force** (q.v.) for anti-terrorist operations

Selection the process undergone by all servicemen seeking to join the SAS. Run by the Regiment's Training Wing (*see* **TW**) at Hereford, it is a mentally and physically gruelling combination of training and endurance tests, divided into phases and run over many weeks. At the end of it, a successful candidate will be **badged** (q.v.), although it will be another two years before he is either accepted or rejected as a full-time member of the Regiment. The two **TA** (q.v.) regiments, 21 and 23 SAS, have their own Selection training programme. Also known, from the Regiment's initials, as 'Savage and Sadistic' (*see* **nicknames**)

SEP surrendered enemy personnel: term used during the campaign in Oman (*see* **Operation Storm** [q.v.]) for *adoo* (q.v.) who gave themselves up to the authorities, many of whom would then join a *firqat* (q.v.)

Service dress uniform worn on parade by all officers. *See also* **No. 2 dress**

Seven Ps, the 'Prior Preparation and Planning Prevent Piss-Poor Performance'. SAS expression, as in 'Don't forget the Seven Ps' said before an operation, or, when something has gone wrong, 'You forgot the Seven Ps'.

SF Special Forces

shaped charge a powerful explosive demolition

charge, the 'shaping' directing the blast in such a way as to cause maximum destruction to the object to be breached or destroyed

shemagh Arab headdress cloth; also called a *keffiyeh*. SAS patrols operating in desert conditions have almost always worn shemaghs, from the earliest days of the Regiment during the Second World War

SIB Special Investigations Branch of the Corps of Royal Military Police

sigint signals intelligence: information about an enemy, target etc. gained from monitoring wireless transmissions, code-breaking, direction-finding, etc. *See also* **elint; humint**

sippers sharing your **brew** (q.v.) (naval; from the Falklands campaign)

sitrep situation report

slot, to to kill, esp. by shooting. *See also* **banjo; stitch**

SLR self-loading rifle: 7.62mm semi-automatic

magazine-fed rifle designed by the Belgian FN arms concern. The standard-issue rifle of the British Army, by which it was designated L1A1, until the introduction of the **SA80** (q.v.) in the 1980s, the British version was hampered by the fact that it could fire only single shots, and by its length and weight; the almost identical FNs used by the Argentinians in the Falklands were fully automatic. Known to soldiers as the 'slur', for obvious reasons

SNCO/JNCO senior/junior non-commissioned officer

SOPs standing operational procedures: instructions issued in the British Army as guidelines, for instance by directing staff (*see* **DS**) or regimental headquarters (*see* **RHQ**), and designed to cover widely differing circumstances a soldier or soldiers might encounter

souk Arab market

SP team Special Projects team: the Regiment's

counter-terrorist team, formed by each of the four **Sabre Squadrons** (q.v.) in rotation, serving in the role for roughly six months at a time, and based in the UK. It is divided into two sub-units, Red and Blue Teams

'Spargan' SAS approximation of the Russian name Shpagin, a term used for a Soviet-designed and built 12.7mm belt-fed, air-cooled heavy machine-gun, usually tripod mounted. The weapon's actual designation is D.Sh.K M1938/46, the first part of the abbreviation standing for the joint designers, Degtyarev and Shpagin, and the 'K' indicating 'heavy'

sparrowfart dawn, or very early in the morning. From the colloquial English expression, 'to be up before a sparrow farts'

splice the mainbrace, to general order given in the Royal Navy to issue a ration or extra ration of alcohol, usually in celebration or to mark an event (naval; from the Falklands campaign)

Spyglass a compact, hand-held night-vision device that operates by thermal imagery, picking up heat signatures from people, vehicle engines, animals etc.

squadron orders specific orders issued by **RHQ** (q.v.) to squadrons and pinned up on the squadron notice board. *See also* **Part 1 orders**

Squadrons *see* **Sabre Squadrons**

SSM(1) squadron sergeant-major, a **WO2** (q.v.)

SSM (2) surface-to-surface missile

stag sentry duty: to be 'on stag', or 'doing stag', means to carry out sentry duty during operations or on exercise

stand to/stand down to 'stand to' is to adopt a state of readiness and alertness at first and last light, anticipating an enemy; troops may also be stood to at any time if a threat materializes. If no threat develops, the men are 'stood down'

standby squadron while one SAS squadron in rotation forms the **SP team** (q.v.), usually for a six-month period, a second acts as standby squadron, also in rotation and for roughly the same period. In practice this means that all the standby squadron's weapons and equipment are kept ready for immediate deployment, while its personnel can and will be recalled from wherever they may be if the squadron is deployed

staple belt blue webbing belt purchased (compulsorily) by all SAS members; the circular chrome-plated buckle is embossed with the regimental **badge** of winged dagger and **motto** (qq.v.). Generally worn with **working dress** (q.v.)

stick army – and especially **Para** (q.v.) – term for a group of parachutists who will jump together

Stinger US-designed and built, shoulder-launched **SAM** (q.v.): utilizing a passive infrared homing system and equipped with an IFF (identification-friend-or-foe) device, Stinger is a 'fire-and-forget' weapon, meaning that once the missile has locked on to a target the operator does not have to guide it. Introduced in the US in 1981, it was used with success by the SAS in the Falklands (*see* **Pucara**), and was carried by SAS patrols in the Gulf War

Stirling Lines a former Royal Artillery barracks in Hereford, which became 22 SAS's headquarters in 1960. Originally called Bradbury Lines (Bradbury was a Gunner **VC** [(1) q.v.]), it was renamed Stirling Lines after the Regiment's founder, David **Stirling** (q.v.), in 1980, when a new barracks was built on the site. In 2000 22 SAS moved to a new purpose-built barracks in Hereford and the old site was sold

Stirling, Lieutenant-Colonel Sir David, DSO, OBE having enlisted in the Scots Guards, Stirling was serving with the Commandos in North Africa in June 1941 when he bluffed his way into an audience with the C-in-C Middle

East. He persuaded General Auchinleck to enlist himself and 65 others to form 'L Detachment' of a mythical 'Special Air Service Brigade' (the name was chosen to confuse German intelligence) for missions behind enemy lines. The first operation, in November 1941, proved a disaster – only 22 out of 60 parachutists survived. Thereafter Stirling decided to use vehicles for deep-penetration raids. He and his unit were spectacularly successful, destroying many German aircraft and sabotaging installations and equipment. In August 1942 L Detachment was formally established as 1 Special Air Service Regiment, under Stirling's command. During an operation in Tunisia in 1943, however, Stirling was captured. He escaped, but was recaptured and sent to a PoW camp in Italy, from which he escaped four more times. Eventually he was sent him to Colditz in Poland, only to be released in May 1945.

Meanwhile the SAS, now comprising two regiments and the **SBS** (q.v.), continued to serve in Italy, the Aegean, the Adriatic, France and Germany, playing a leading part in disrupting enemy communications until its disbandment in October 1945. After the war Stirling went to live in East Africa, but returned to Britain in 1959, where he became involved in television. Although he never interfered in the re-formed Regiment's affairs, in 1967 he founded an organization that employed ex-SAS members as bodyguards and advisers to governments or rulers abroad, mainly the Middle East. He resigned in 1972, but maintained his interest in the Regiment and its former members. He suffered hostile press criticism during the 1970s, but SAS successes in the 1980s did much to restore his reputation with the public. He was knighted in 1990, only a few months before his death. Courteous, cultured, modest and self-sufficient, David Stirling's creative vision, leadership and example not only inspired his beloved Regiment, but provided a model that persists to this day. His brother, **Lieutenant-Colonel William Stirling**, also originally from the Scots Guards, joined David in the SAS from No. 62 Commando. In 1942 he established 2 SAS Regiment, which he commanded in North Africa and Italy. He resigned his command in 1944, after a dispute with High Command over the deployment of his unit in the coming invasion of Europe

stitch, to to kill, esp. by shooting – supposedly from the 'stitching' effect of a burst of fire hitting a person. *See also* **banjo; slot**

stun grenade *see* **flash bang**

SUS soldier under sentence

Swift scope a telescopic single-lens monocular – a powerful optical instrument used for observation at long ranges

Swiss Army knife trade name for any of several versions of a multi-function pocket knife, probably the most famous implement of its kind in the world, and immediately recognizable from its red handle inset with a white or silver Swiss cross. Apart from knife blades, top-of-the-range models include scissors, pliers, screwdrivers, openers, saw, tweezers, toothpick, magnifying glass etc., all of which fold up or fit into the handle. Made by Victorinox in Switzerland, it is not an issue item but, as with the **Leatherman** (q.v.), many SAS soldiers buy their own. *See also* **'fighting knife'**

TA Territorial Army. The SAS has two TA regiments, 21 and 23 SAS, which serve as a reserve to be deployed in the event of a major conflict

tab, to to march: SAS and **Para** (q.v.) slang, equivalent to the Royal Marine Commandos' 'yomp'

TACBE tactical beacon: a light and compact surface-to-air rescue beacon, weighing only some 250 grams, which is used to make direct contact with friendly aircraft flying overhead if other means of communication have failed. Its principal disadvantage is that its signals are easily detected by enemy direction-finding equipment. Also known as SARBE (search-and-rescue beacon)

tail-end Charlie the soldier selected to bring up the rear during a march, tasked with protecting the rest of his patrol from attack from behind. *See also* **lead scout**

time pencil chemical timing device used to detonate explosive charges

TLS tactical landing strip for **C-130s** (q.v.) landing on grass, in the desert, etc. *See also* **HLS**

tracer small-arms and, sometimes, heavier-calibre ammunition that illuminates in flight, allowing the firer to adjust his aim. Tracer rounds contain a chemical in the base that burns while the projectile is in flight. Generally one round in five in a magazine or belt is tracer, and such rounds illuminate after 110 metres and burn out at 1100 metres

Trimpack electronic satellite-navigation device, used by SAS patrols in the Gulf campaign. *See also* **GPS**

tube nickname for the British 81mm mortar. *See* **L16**

TW Training Wing: based at Hereford, it is responsible for all SAS training including **Selection** (q.v.)

UAE United Arab Emirates: an independent group of seven emirates on the Persian Gulf, including Abu Dhabi and Dubai. The Regiment maintains a permanent desert-training camp in the UAE, and conducts training exercises and tests in remote parts of the area

ulu SAS term for jungle (from a Malay word

meaning 'upstream); also used by the **Green
Army** (q.v.)

Unimog Mercedes-Benz 4x4 light truck, used as a
support vehicle by SAS mobile patrols. The
name is a contraction of German *Universal
Motorgerät*

US Special Forces nicknamed the 'Green Berets',
America's multi-discipline special-service troops
are trained in many of the skills and techniques
common to the SAS, and the two units maintain
close contacts. *See also* **A Team**; **Delta Force**

VC (1) Victoria Cross: the highest British military
award for gallantry

VC (2) voluntary contribution – 'voluntary' is a
euphemism; this is, in fact, a fine, paid to
squadron funds, imposed on an SAS soldier for
some transgression. If a soldier fails or declines
to pay the VC, he will be charged on an **AF252**
(q.v.); in practice, people invariably take the first
option

VCP vehicle checkpoint. *See also* **IVCP**

wadi Arabic for valley or dried-up watercourse

warrant certificate of rank issued over the signature of the Secretary of State for Defence to all warrant officers, the formal grant of their authority. *See also* **WO1, WO2**

whiteout extreme blizzard conditions

wilco SAS term for someone who is positive, willing, cooperative

winged dagger *see* **badge**

wings SAS parachute wings are unique to the Regiment. Dating from the unit's early days in North Africa during the Second World War, they are thought to have been modelled on a symbolical ibis with outstretched wings copied from a fresco in Shepheard's Hotel, Cairo, with the body of the bird being replaced by a parachute. Until 1957 they were worn on the left breast, but since then have been worn on the right shoulder. *See also* **badge**; **motto**

WO1 Warrant Officer Class 1, usually an **RSM** (q.v.)

WO2 Warrant Office Class 2, in the SAS, usually a squadron sergeant-major (*see* **SSM** [1])

working dress everyday uniform consisting, for the SAS, of lightweight **DPM** (q.v.) tunic and trousers, **staple belt** (q.v.), **beret** (q.v.) and boots

yellow card card carried by all soldiers on duty in Northern Ireland, on which are printed the **ROE** (q.v.)

URGr8! ltle bk of pwr txt ISBN 1-85479-817-0
The Little Book of Cockney Rhyming Slang
ISBN 1-85479-825-1
The Little Book of Gay Gags ISBN 1-85479-590-2
The Little Book of Irish Grannies' Remedies
ISBN 1-85479-828-6
The Little Book of Scottish Grannies' Remedies
ISBN 1-85479-829-4
The Little Book of Irish Wit and Wisdom
ISBN 1-85479-827-8
The Little Book of Scottish Wit and Wisdom
ISBN 1-85479-826-X

Postage and packing outside the UK:
Europe: add 20% of retail price
Rest of the world: add 30% of retail price

To order any Michael O'Mara book please call our
credit-card hotline: **020 8324 5652**

Michael O'Mara Bookshop, BVCD
32–34 Park Royal Road, London NW10 7LN